Making Money Series

How to Choose a Good

Network Marketing Company

By A. A. Sarkiss

No unauthorized photocopying

All rights reserved. No part of this publication may be reproduced, stored in a retrieval system, or transmitted, in any form or by any means, electronic, mechanical, photocopying, recording, or otherwise, without the prior written permission of the author.

This book is subject to the condition that it shall not, by way of trade or otherwise, be lent, resold, hired out or otherwise circulated without the author's prior consent in any form of binding or cover other than that in which it is published and without a similar condition including this condition being imposed on the subsequent purchaser.

Copyright@2014 A. A. Sarkiss

Printed by CreateSpace, An Amazon.com Company

Available from Amazon.com, CreateSpace.com and other retail outlets

Available on Kindle and other devices

Table of Contents

Introduction	4
Chapter One: What is direct selling?	7
Chapter Two: Background, Concepts and Perceptions	10
Chapter Three: Company Profile	13
Chapter Four: The Plan	18
Chapter Five: The Products	26
Chapter Six: Training and Support	28
Chapter Seven: Money	30
Chapter Eight: Other Considerations	32
Question Checklist	34

Introduction

Prior to June 2010, I had some knowledge of the network marketing industry but not enough to want to join any of the existing companies. I had been working at a traditional job for years and had started feeling like I was going nowhere fast. Sure, I had the experience, the degrees, the knowledge and the work ethics that got me quickly up the corporate ladder. However, the higher I went up the ladder, the more the responsibilities and the more I realized that, at the end of the day, I was expendable; I was a mere expense! Very few corporations view their staff otherwise. Once I realized this, I yearned for something that would take me out of the rat race and into the realm of freedom; freedom to work when I wanted to, where I wanted to and with whoever I wanted to. Basically, to be my own boss and work towards my dreams as opposed to the dreams of the corporation.

So I was psychologically ready for change when an old friend met me one afternoon and told me she had recently joined a business that was very different from what I had been accustomed to. I agreed to a business meeting and, a couple of days later, we were sipping coffee and talking business. I sat there listening to every word she said. And it was only fifteen minutes into her presentation that I decided it was what I had been searching for. Every aspect of her presentation spoke to me; financial freedom and personal freedom both rolled into one very interesting and inspiring business plan. I agreed to join as soon as she had put her pen down. My only question was whether I could join right there and then but start working at it a couple of weeks later due to an upcoming business trip. The answer was music to my ears; "By the time you're back from your business trip, I will have probably placed other people below you in the network."

So I chose a product, joined on the spot, went on my business trip and, sure enough, found other people had been placed below me in the network by the time I started working at it. But being my finicky self, I felt I needed to do some research in case I was asked some questions, by my future prospects, about the industry. I did a thorough research and found that I had joined one of the best network marketing companies.

As days and months went by, I made a lot more money than the amount I had used to join but, by then, the market had started filling up with tens of different network marketing companies, some of which were illegal. Many people fell into the trap of joining illegal companies because most people, just like me, join first and do the research later. Some don't do the research at all and they wake up one day to find that their company had been closed down. So I made it my job to tell people how to find out which companies not to join. I consider myself lucky that when I was given a presentation to join a network marketing company, it was actually a good company. But many people were not as lucky. And this brings me to the reason why I decided to write this book. Every person should be able to have what I have; the knowledge to choose a good network marketing company. So let's begin.

Chapter One

What is direct selling?

Before choosing which network marketing company suits you most, you need to have a deeper understanding of the industry.

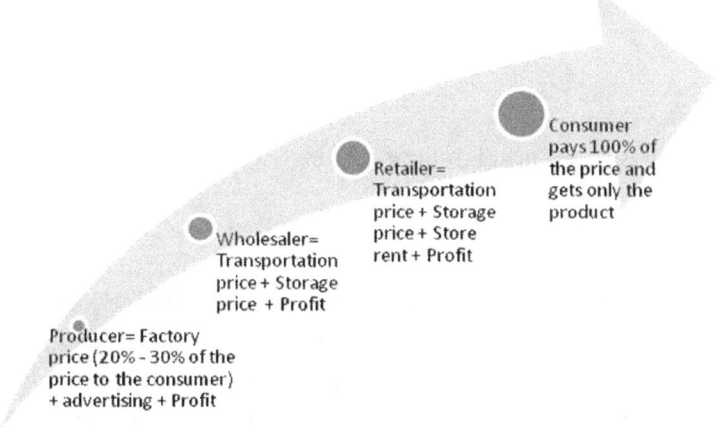

Figure 1: Traditional Selling

Traditional selling is when there are mediators between the producer and the consumer/end user. The product price starts off at the production cost; 20% to 30% of its market price. Then the cost of advertising and the producer's profit are added to it. The wholesaler then adds his own profit as well as any expenses he suffered in the process including transporting and storing the product. The retailer then adds his own profit as well as any expenses he suffered including transporting and storing the product and the shop rent. The

7

consumer finally pays for the product at 70% more on its original production cost and receives just the product. This is the way most of us have bought most of our things, whether it is our food, electric appliances etc.

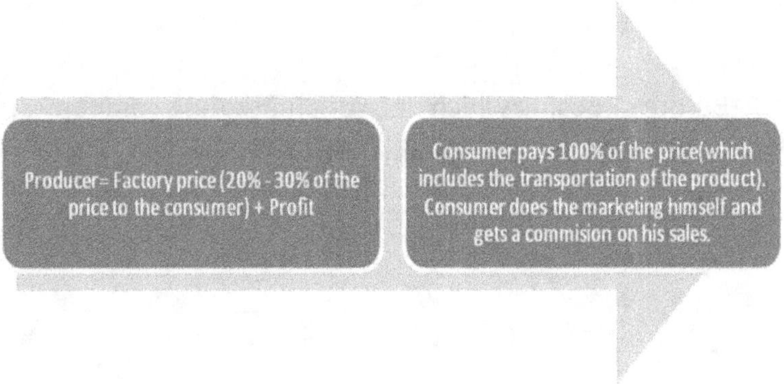

Producer= Factory price (20% - 30% of the price to the consumer) + Profit

Consumer pays 100% of the price (which includes the transportation of the product). Consumer does the marketing himself and gets a commision on his sales.

Figure 2: Direct Selling

Direct selling is the selling of products directly to consumers away from a fixed retail location. Direct selling includes sales made through the party plan, one-on-one demonstrations, and other personal contact arrangements. A textbook definition is: "The direct personal presentation, demonstration, and sale of products and services to consumers, usually in their homes or at their jobs." In short, direct selling is the cutting out of the middle men, including the wholesaler, the retailer, the advertising, the marketing and all the non-essential transportation. The consumer still pays 100% of the price which includes the transportation of the product to him. The consumer does the marketing himself and gets a commission on his sales. So, in effect, the consumer buys a product he would have bought anyway but instead of getting just a product, he gets a product and a lucrative business at a relatively low cost and without the hassles of starting his own business.

Direct selling is different from direct marketing because it is about salespersons reaching and dealing directly with clients. Direct marketing is about business organizations seeking a relationship with their customers without going through an agent or a retail outlet. Direct selling often, but not always, uses multi-level marketing; the salesperson is paid for selling and for sales made by people he recruits rather than single-level marketing; the salesperson is paid only for the sales he makes himself.

Direct selling is a low risk, high return home-based business. Working for yourself, whenever you want with whoever you want and without having to commute are parts of the very nature of this industry.

As more people see the benefits of direct selling, more network marketing companies are established. Even some traditional companies are trying to adopt a similar system to entice their staff to work harder.

Chapter Two

Background, Concepts and Perceptions

Most international direct selling associations are represented in the World Federation of Direct Selling Associations (WFDSA). These trade associations are in the United States, United Kingdom, Australia, Malaysia, Singapore, and New Zealand.

www.wfdsa.org

According to the WFDSA, consumers benefit from direct selling because of the convenience and service it provides, including personal demonstration and explanation of products, home delivery, and generous satisfaction guarantees. In contrast to franchising, the cost for an individual to start an independent direct selling business is typically very low with little or no required inventory. In addition, most direct selling associations around the world require their member companies to abide by a code of conduct towards a fair partnership with customers and salespersons.

The WFDSA reports that in 2007 its 59 regional member associations accounted for more than US$114 billion in retail sales, through the activities of more than 62 million independent salespersons. The United States Direct Selling Association (DSA) reports that in 2000, 55% of adult Americans had at some time purchased goods or services from a direct selling representative and 20% reported that they were a direct selling representative.

www.dsa.org

The DSA was formed in Binghamton, New York in 1910. It was called the Agents Credit Association. It was reorganized in 1914 and re-named the National Association of Agency Companies. In 1917, the name was changed to the National Association of Agency and Mail Order Companies, but the name was changed back in 1920. In 1924, the Association established its headquarters in Winona, Minnesota. In 1925, the association was again reorganized and renamed the National Association of Direct Selling Companies. The list of active members numbered 80. In 1968, a final reorganization gave the association its current name and the headquarters moved to Washington, D.C., where it has remained since.

Currently, the DSA has approximately 200 member companies, including many well-known brand names. The Association's mission is to protect the effectiveness of member companies and the independent salespersons and to ensure that the marketing and the direct sales are done with the highest level of business ethics. Every member company pledges to abide by the standards set in the DSA's Code of Ethics and procedures as a condition of admission and continuing membership in the DSA.

Another credible, highly respected association is the Direct Selling Association of Singapore (DSAS).

www.dsas.org.sg

DSAS was founded in 1977 and took a stand against high-pressure sales tactics and other forms of malpractice. It introduced a Code of Ethics and made it compulsory for every member company to strictly adhere to it. DSAS has hosted several direct selling events and seminars since its establishment. Its objectives include promoting high standard of merchandising and servicing practices and protecting the needs of its member companies and those of the public.

Perceptions

By 2012, 13 million Americans and 55 million people worldwide were working as Independent Representatives in the direct selling industry. Because of its growth rate and ability to withstand economic collapses, the industry has been dubbed "The business of the 21st Century" and "The recession proof business".

Forbes Magazine, a leading source for reliable business news and financial information, has featured numerous articles about the industry and some of its leading companies. Time Warner, the American multinational media corporation, and Sir Richard Branson, the British Billionaire investor, have both invested in this business. Donald Trump, the American billionaire investor, and Robert Kiyosaki, the American millionaire investor, motivational speaker and self-help author both recommend network marketing. The American billionaire investor and philanthropist, Warren Buffet calls it, "The best investment I ever made."

Chapter Three

Company Profile

When deciding which network marketing company to join, you should research the company itself. Inevitably, companies will not publicly share their shortcomings. However, knowing what to look for will save you a great deal of time and money.

Age 5+ Years

Even though every company was once a young company and everyone should be given a fair chance, nowadays with so many companies to choose from and worldwide recessions resulting in companies filing for bankruptcy, it is vital to stick to this rule of thumb: choose a network marketing company that is at least 5 years old. The reason behind this is that all newly established companies have many ups and downs. A huge number of companies close down in the first 3 years of their lives. So the last thing you want is to have your money in a company that is still on shaky grounds. If the company has reached the 5 year threshold you can feel confident that it will continue to flourish.

Word of Mouth

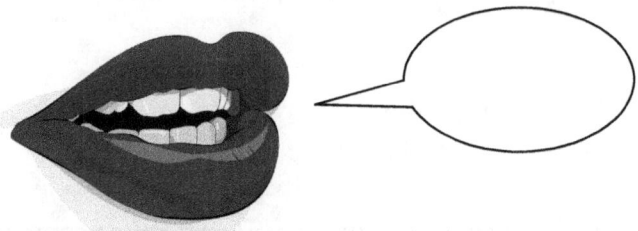

Network marketing companies depend on word of mouth for their marketing so, needless to say, a good network marketing company will do anything and everything to keep its name clean. Some people try to abuse this by trying to sue these companies, hoping that the companies would succumb to their threats and pay them off to get them off their backs. Good companies; however, will not give in to threats and will fight it out in courts. So it is vital that you research the lawsuits well and find out what the final verdicts were.

Another point to keep in mind is that because of the nature of network marketing, representatives work independently. This has resulted in some representatives using people's ignorance to their advantage. There have been reported cases of representatives being dishonest; selling the products without explaining the business plan attached to it. In other cases, representatives would buy the products themselves and sell them at a much higher price. What you should look for is how the company responded. Good companies close the representative's account and look at ways to ensure it doesn't happen again. Depending on the situation, some companies tighten restrictions at the market where the incident happened. Some companies have started issuing IDs for their representatives. In other cases, a more limited product range is offered at that market.

Another issue you need to be aware of is the use of the internet to badmouth people and companies. If you type in any name of any network marketing company followed by the word 'scam' you would, inevitably, find someone somewhere who claims to have been scammed by this company. So using this method to research the company only makes your task harder. In my search for truth, I've started conversations with such people and, after a few basic questions, knew for a fact who had been scammed and who hadn't. You'll need to dig deep with questioning whether they contacted the company with their problem, whether they checked their email to see if the company had replied, whether they had actually done some work to deserve the money they believe they should have got. I have found that some of these people claiming to have been scammed never even joined the company they were claiming to have scammed them.

An easier way to double check whether a network marketing company is legitimate is to check whether that company is on the list of companies in the different direct selling association websites mentioned in Chapter Two. If the company is not listed on any of them, choose another company. If the company is listed, you can rest assured that the law suits, bad publicity or otherwise about the company are unfounded. Remember, all listed companies must adhere to the Code of Ethics or else they are no longer members of the WFDSA, the DSA or the DSAS.

Growth and Progress

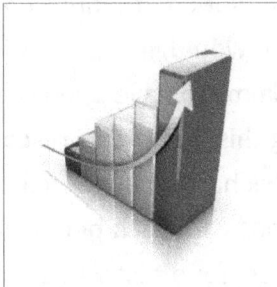

It is vital you research the company and its history. How has it grown since its establishment? Has it been slow and steady? Has it had leaps? How has the media taken to it? Has it been featured or written about in financial newspapers or magazines? Has it been mentioned in Forbes? Has it been endorsed by celebrities? The reason for the question regarding celebrities has nothing to do with whether it's trendy to join but rather the fact that celebrities and successful people are careful not to couple their names with something that could backfire. With all this growth, just how good is their website? Can it withstand a huge increase in customers? Is it updated and maintained regularly?

Globalization

With the world ever becoming smaller, the last thing you want to join is a networking company that cannot go places, literally. A good network marketing company is primarily online. Online doesn't just mean that it has a website. Online means that you can easily access their training, go through their catalog, sign up new people, and place orders etc online. It means your possible prospects can be where ever the internet can reach and not just to the borders of your own country. It also means that you can be anywhere and do business. You don't have to be stuck in a country for the rest of your life just because your business is there. It means you can be sitting on a beach doing business. It means you don't have to be hoarding samples of your products where ever you go. If you choose a network marketing company that requires only a laptop and an access to the internet, then you've got it made; true freedom!

Chapter Four

The Plan

In 1970, less than 5% of the DSA's members were multi-level marketing companies. By 2011, the DSA's membership had grown to include nearly 200 companies, more than 90% of which were multi-level marketing companies. So most network marketing companies are multi-level marketing; meaning that the independent representative is paid for his own sales and for sales made by people he recruits rather than single-level marketing where the independent representative is paid only for the sales he makes himself. Whether single or multi-level, the latter of course being the better one, you should pay close attention to the plan. The plan is the way you will be compensated for your work so you need to pay special attention to several factors.

Different Kinds of plans

Under the umbrella of network marketing, there are many kinds of plans; some legal, some illegal, some designed to help you make money and some designed to make the company more money. How can you tell the difference? It's all in the plan. While you are reading the plan or being presented it, decide which of the following plans best describes the company.

Ponzi Scheme (pyramiding): This is the only illegal one. There has been a move not to name it under the umbrella of network marketing. Rightly so! But for the sake of explaining what it is, I am adding it here. Its features are as follows:

1- You will not find it listed at www.wfdsa.org
2- There is no product or the product is something you can otherwise get for free such as an email address.
3- It hasn't been established for long. Most Ponzi schemes don't last more than 2 years. That's due to the fact that once they are caught, they are closed down.
4- The people higher up the pyramid make more money than those lower down the pyramid, regardless of their work and effort.
5- In most cases, cash is their only method of payment since they are not a legal company and cannot send/receive money via official financial institutions.

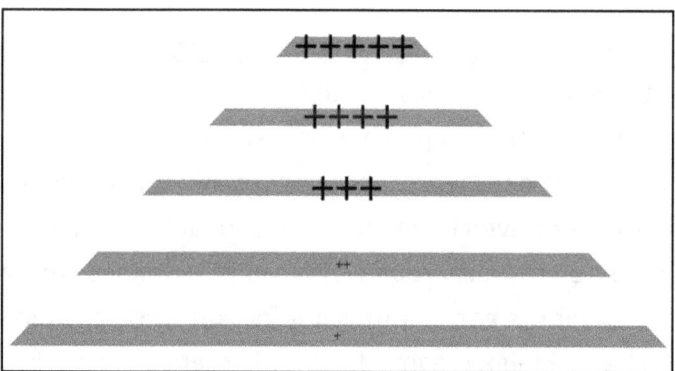

Figure 3: Ponzi Scheme

Chain: Even though this plan is actually legal, it is definitely best avoided. There is a real product involved but Chain Plans work as follows. A buys a product and signs up B. B signs up C etc. However, if C decides not to do any work, both A and B would have to buy another product in order to re-join the business and start the chain again. As shown in Figure 4, each person leads to the next. If anyone stops, the chain is broken and everyone has to start again. Very few network marketing companies use this plan.

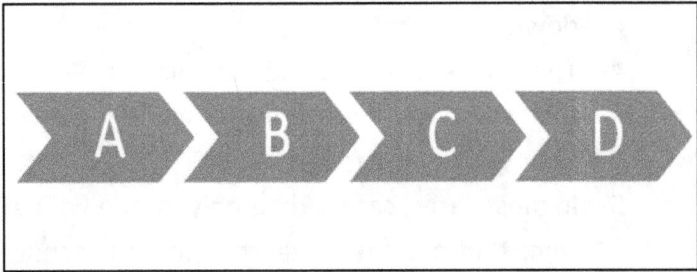

Figure 4: Chain

Traditional MLM (multi- level marketing): Most network marketing companies use this plan. This plan seems to lend itself more to very personal marketing; door to door, marketing parties etc. So expect to either carry or store samples or even large quantities. So, unless you are prepared to walk around with samples or have storage space for the goods, this is not for you. Their products tend to be make-up, creams, food and other consumable items to help keep the business going by making the purchaser keep buying the products. The plan is simple; you become part of their sales force, you sell their products, get a discount on what you personally order and get a commission on what you sell. When you make the order, you also collect it or it is sent to you and you deliver it to the purchaser. In most cases, the purchaser is only a purchaser and not a business partner. This is because you actually receive lower commissions on what your teams sell as opposed to what you sell directly. So if you decide to have a sales team working below you, you do get a commission but it diminishes the more layers you have below you until it reaches a level whereby you receive virtually no money. This kind of plan keeps you working because once you stop working it, it stops generating money. So you have to keep working and finding new purchasers.

Another result of traditional MLM is shown in Figure 5. A joins the business and directly sells to his clients to get the highest possible commission. Then A decides to have teams. But because the more layers he has the less he gets, A decides to put each team on a different 'leg' of the network; thereby increasing his commission. This is good for A but not for his leaders (B, C, D…) who only get training help from A but, of course, no financial help.

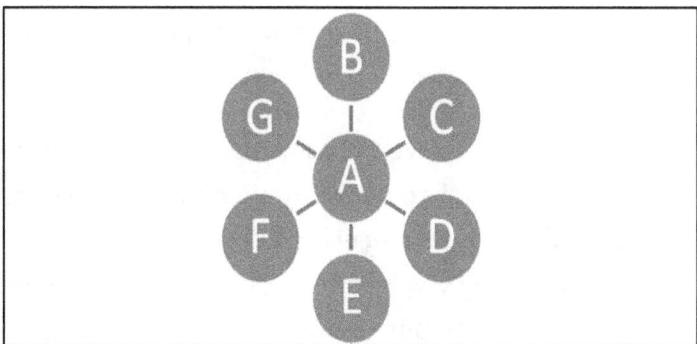

Figure 5: Traditional MLM

Most traditional MLM also have a deadline to reach a certain target. If you don't reach it before the deadline, you receive nothing. For example, for every 5 new sign ups before the end of the month, you receive X amount of money. If you sign up 9, you receive the X amount of money for 5 sign ups and you don't receive any money for the remaining 4 sign ups.

Moreover, this kind of network marketing doesn't easily lend itself to crossing borders unless the company has a branch there and you are physically there. But once you are there, you basically lose your old clients.

<u>Binary MLM:</u> These network marketing companies have solved the issues limiting the success of those who join them. Binary means you have only two 'legs' and you get paid when you reach a balance of 3 or 6 purchasers on each leg; the number varies according to the company (See Figure 6). You get paid for direct selling and for sales made by the people you recruit. The commission is stable, not diminishing, no matter how many layers you have on each leg.

Moreover, you receive the same commission whether or not the person you sell to decides to join the business with you. But if he doesn't, you receive the business value of what he bought; meaning you increase your 'shares' in the business. However, both the purchaser and you benefit if he decides to join the business. For him, he has a good plan B when there is a recession/if he is made redundant/if he loses his traditional business etc and he gets a discount for every item he decides to buy for himself later. However, unlike traditional MLM, he doesn't have to keep purchasing to stay in the business. Your benefit is that you gain a business partner who, if he decides to work at it, helps you make money. But, unlike the Chain Plan, if he joins but doesn't work at it, you don't lose anything and you don't have to start again. You just place someone in that same leg below him. The great thing about this is that if he later decides to work at it, he'll find he has one very long leg and he would work at the other leg to make the balance in order to get paid and so you, too, get paid for the work he has done. Basically, it's a win-win situation. The fact that you have only 2 legs means that you keep placing people below one another so the help you give your teams is financial as well.

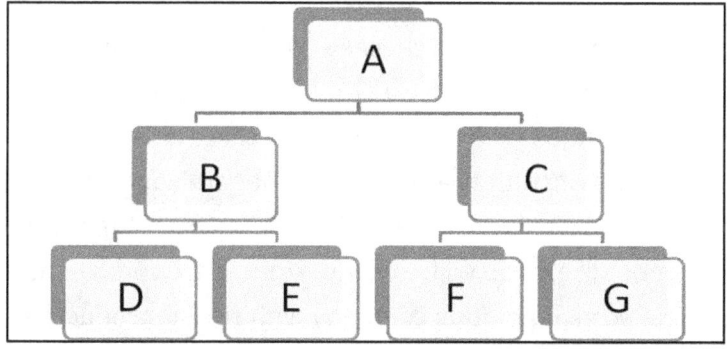

Figure 6: Binary MLM

Because there is no need to keep purchasing, most Binary MLM companies have non-consumable products as their main products. Moreover, most are internet based so the product details, the registering of new purchasers/business partners and the orders are online. The companies do all the paperwork for you and the product is shipped to the purchaser's address by courier. So you don't need to store or carry around samples and you don't need to follow up on orders. If you have access to a laptop/personal computer and the internet, you can be anywhere and still be able to do this business well. The financial results of this one point are massive because you can have several business partners in different countries. If one market collapses for any reason, other markets cover you (and cover the collapsed market if the collapsed market is above the other markets). So due to the nature of Binary MLM, the cost of delay can be massive. If a person delays the decision to join, he could have a massive market above him as opposed to below him if he had taken the decision to join earlier.

Legal issues

Assuming you have checked whether the company is listed at www.wfdsa.org, you also need to double check your own legal status with the company. Is there a contract of sorts? What constitutes a contract? What are your rights? What are the company expectations? The better the company, the more likely you will not be permitted to work at another network marketing company with similar products at the same time. Where is the company based? What happens if a product is faulty? Can you stock the products if you wanted to? Can you advertise if you wanted to? Whether you want to or not is not the issue but the idea is that you need to have that knowledge so you don't make a mistake and discover it cost you your account with the company.

Other issues

In general, you need to look out for certain things in a plan. How easy is it to understand? Is it straight forward or can only a genius figure out how much he would be paid? Is it a flexible plan? By flexible, you need to look at whether anyone could do it. The last thing you want is to join a plan that is good for only one gender, one culture, one age group, one walk of life etc. If it is a limiting plan then it will be more difficult for you to market it. Ask yourself how many of those you know would benefit from the plan. Can it be done as a part time job or would you have to drop everything just to make some money out of it? If you had to travel, can it travel with you? If you had to take time off, would you lose money? Does it have the capacity to one day make you money while you sleep?

Chapter Five

The Products

Network marketing companies have become so numerous that virtually every single item you can think of is sold by at least one network marketing company: perfumes, make-up, shampoos, tea, coffee, clothes, flowers, watches, holidays, online courses, seasonal products etc. Therefore it is important to select a company that is choosy about its products.

Unique and exclusive

A good company has its own range of products that are unique to it. This means that while there may be other similar products on the market, their product has something that makes it stand out high above the others. This definitely helps the marketability of their products. The exclusivity of the product ensures that you don't put in the effort only to find your client has bought the very same product from a nearby store.

Useful

Ask yourself how useful the products would be to yourself and the people you know. The more people you can think of that may buy it, the more useful it actually is. Inevitably, the more useful a product is, the more people will buy it.

Consumables vs. non-consumables

As a rule of thumb, while consumable products generate multiple sales, long lasting non-consumable products yield higher commissions. The ideal situation is a company that has both kinds of products, some long lasting to give you higher commissions and some consumables to give you a regular stream of income.

Variety and increase

Having a variety of products enables you to approach different kinds of clients. You should also check the company's history to see how often it adds new products. This shows how forward thinking the company is. A company that keeps improving itself and its product range is a company that is in it to stay.

Chapter Six

Training and Support

To join a network marketing company, you don't need to have any specialized knowledge or previous experience. However, this does not mean that you don't need training once you join. Having training and support available is a strong factor for your success. Most companies provide training for their representatives. However, knowing the extent of that training is vital. How much training will you get? Is the training an on-going procedure? Will you have to travel in order to get trained? Will you have to buy their training material? Will you have a 'mentor' or will you just learn from your mistakes? I have found that some people fall into the trap of having to pay for the training or to travel at their own expense. This is, of course, on top of what they paid initially. This, understandably, makes people feel cheated. So it is crucial to find out exactly the kind of training and support you will get and whether that will cost you before you join a network marketing company. Moreover, keep in mind that different people learn at different speed and some prefer to have self-study material available to them. Remember that the decision you take for yourself is also the decision you take for those who join the business with you. So if the company you chose sells their training material and you are fine with that, those who join with you may or may not be fine with that.

Chapter Seven

Money

Needless to say, this is one of the most important aspects to research. Unbelievably, many join a network marketing company without knowing how they will get paid and some later find out it is truly cumbersome for them. There are no right and wrong methods of payment. What is important is having the knowledge about everything before you join a company.

The payment system: With several payment systems such as direct bank deposits, PayPal, checks etc, a company should have no problems finding the most suitable methods to pay you. Find out the following:

1- The method(s) used to pay you. The more methods used the better. Again think of those who will join with you. Would the payment method(s) suit them all?
2- The method(s) used to enroll clients. If only cash is used even though it is a legitimate company, some people might find that suspicious. If only credit cards are accepted, then it may not be suitable for

everyone. You may live in a country where most people have credit cards but not all countries have been completely converted to credit cards.
3- How long it takes to get paid. From the time you make a sale to the time you get paid for that sale can make a huge difference to you at first so it is important to ask.
4- How often you get paid. Is it monthly? Weekly?
5- If their website is used for payments, how secure is it? The last thing you want is to use a credit card only to find a hacker just got a hold of its information.
6- Which currency is used to pay you?
7- When do you get your first check? Some network marketing companies hold your first check for a certain number of weeks so be sure to ask if this is the case with the company you are joining.
8- Can you start making money straight away? This question is related to what I mentioned earlier about targets that some Traditional MLM companies have. Will you have to reach a certain target before they pay you?

Chapter Eight

Other Considerations

Now that you have settled on which network marketing company to join, you'll need to bear some other things in mind.

Choosing the network

How do you feel about the person who just presented the business to you? Could you work with him? Do you communicate well? Is he the kind of person who wants to succeed or will he count on your effort for his success? At the end of the day, these things matter only at the beginning. Once you understand the business and how it works, you can work in a way to limit any conflicts. However, while the nature of network marketing prevents major conflicts from taking place, it is important to note that there will still be some conflicts related to differences in personality. But conflicts of interest and other major conflicts found in a traditional working place are rarely found in network marketing.

Choosing the prospects

Whether one should be choosy about who purchases from them depends on what they are looking for. Of course, there is no need to be choosy if you are looking for people to only buy your products. But if you are looking for business partners, you may want to be choosy. Again, how well do you communicate? Is he results oriented? Is he willing to learn? What is he hoping to achieve by joining the business? Is he ambitious? Is he committed to his success? How committed? How many hours a week is he willing to use to reach his goals? At the end of the day, there is no boss in network marketing so you can not actually tell him how many hours a week he should work etc. But you may want to have a network that is 100% active and results oriented. And in that case, you may want to know just how committed he is.

Finally, is he honest? Does he keep his promises? Would he exaggerate just to close a deal? Dishonesty in network marketing is a real problem as the industry relies on word of mouth as previously mentioned. The last thing you want is a dishonest addition to your network. But do keep in mind that some people do change for the better. So you may want to give him a chance to change before you allow him into your network.

Question Checklist

Network marketing has produced more millionaires than any other business. Experts believe that every 10 years 100,000 new millionaires are born out of this industry. But these millionaires don't get there by chance. It requires choosing a good company and recruiting good business partners. This is followed by having the passion, the dedication and the consistency to reach the goals you set out for yourself.

This question checklist can be used as a quick guide to what to look for when choosing a good network marketing company. For most questions, there are no right or wrong answers. The important issue here is having the knowledge in order to choose the company that is good for you.

1- Is the company listed at www.wfdsa.org, www.dsa.org or www.dsas.org.sg?
2- When was the company established?
3- How has it grown since its establishment?
4- Has it been featured or written about in financial newspapers or magazines?
5- Has it been endorsed by celebrities?
6- Is their website updated and maintained regularly?
7- How useful is their website?

8- Will you have to carry or store samples or products?

9- Is it a Chain, Traditional MLM or Binary MLM?

10- Is it a diminishing commission?

11- Will you have to keep buying to stay in the business?

12- Are there set targets?

13- What happens if someone in your network stops working at it?

14- What is your legal status with the company?

15- What are your rights?

16- What are the company expectations?

17- Where is the company based?

18- What happens if a product is faulty?

19- Can you stock the products if you wanted to?

20- Can you advertise if you wanted to?

21- Is the plan easy to understand? Is it flexible?

22- Can it be done as a part time job?

23- If you had to travel, can it travel with you?

24- If you had to take time off, would you lose money?

25- Does it have the capacity to one day make you money while you sleep?

26- Are their products unique, exclusive, useful, (non)consumables?

27- How various is the product range? Has it increased since the company was established?

28- Is there training and support?

29- Will you have to travel to get trained?

30- Will you pay for the training?

31- Will you pay for training material?

32- Will you have a mentor?

33- What are the payment methods?

34- What are the payment methods used to enroll clients?

35- How long does it take to get paid for a sale?

36- How often do you get paid?

37- If the website is used for payments, how secure is it?

38- Which currency is used to pay you?

39- When do you get your first check?

40- Can you start making money straight away?

41- Will you have to reach a certain target before they pay you?

42- How do you feel about the person who just presented the business to you?

43- Give your prospect 1 point for each: communicative, results oriented, willing to learn, ambitious, committed to his success, active, keeps his promises, and does not exaggerate. Now add 2 points if s/he is honest. 5 or more out of 10 is a good start.

www.ingramcontent.com/pod-product-compliance
Lightning Source LLC
Chambersburg PA
CBHW070726180526
45167CB00004B/1640